The FRIENDLY SHARK

A story for all kids at school who enjoy learning exciting new things and making new friends

ORLA KELLY
PUBLISHING

Phares El Essawi

Copyright © 2020 Phares El Essawi

ISBN 978-1-912328-82-6

All intellectual property rights, including copyright, design right and publishing rights, rest with the author. No part of this book may be copied, reproduced, stored or transmitted in any way including any written, electronic, recording, or photocopying without written permission of the author. Published in Ireland by Orla Kelly Publishing.

Our differences are what make the world beautiful; just like the deep blue sea which is full of different fish, plants and sea creatures living together.

Imagine if there was only one type of fish in the sea – how boring would that be?

The world is rich because we are different. Let's embrace our differences and live together happily without judgement.

Dedicated to our beautiful wee man, Adam, who has inspired us to be the best parents and people we can be.

Seahorse lives with his parents, Mammy Seahorse and Daddy Seahorse, in the deep blue sea.

Seahorse has many friends. Their names are Starfish, Jellyfish, Goldfish and Dolphin.

They all go to school together. There, they learn exciting new things and have a lot of fun playing together during break-time.

Last week, they learnt about all the different types of plants in the sea. Then, they had a sports day. They all played fun games together.

One day on his way to school, Seahorse heard a lot of shouting and screaming. He didn't know what was going on. Then suddenly, he saw his friends swimming away from their school really fast.

Seahorse shouted, "What's wrong guys? Are you not going to school today?"

They looked at him with fear in their eyes.

Starfish said, "A big shark is standing outside our school, and he is going to eat us all!"

Seahorse turned around and swam home really fast. He did not want to be eaten up by a shark.

The next day, the same thing happened. On his way to school, Seahorse heard a lot of shouting and yelling. Then he saw his friends swimming home really fast again.

Seahorse said, "What's wrong guys? Is the shark back?"

Jellyfish looked back at him and said, "The big, angry shark is back. He is standing outside our school ready to gobble us up!"

Seahorse turned around and swam home again. He was very sad because he was missing another day of school. Seahorse loved school. He enjoyed learning new things and playing with his friends during break-time.

When Daddy Seahorse came home from work, he noticed that Seahorse had been crying. He asked him, "What's wrong, Seahorse? Why are you so sad?"

Seahorse told him he hadn't been to school in two days, and he really missed school and his friends.

Daddy Seahorse looked at him and asked, "Why have you not been to school? Is everything ok? I know how much fun you have at school and how much you love it."

Seahorse said, "A big angry shark is standing outside our school, and he wants to gobble us up!"

Daddy Seahorse said, "How do you know that he wants to eat you?"

Seahorse said, "Starfish told me."

Daddy Seahorse looked at Mammy Seahorse and smiled. He turned to Seahorse and said, "Seahorse, do you remember your first day at school? How the other children were scared of you?"

Seahorse said, "Yes Daddy but I wasn't scary at all. I just wanted to go to school to learn new things and make friends."

Daddy said, "You are right, Seahorse, and maybe Shark also wants to go to school and make new friends. Did you try to talk to Shark? It would be best if you didn't judge anyone without even giving them a chance. I am sure if you spoke to him, he will turn out to be a very friendly shark."

Seahorse said, "You are right, Daddy. Tomorrow I will talk to Shark. We should never judge anyone without getting to know them."

The next day on his way to school the same thing happened. Seahorse's friends were screaming and swimming home really fast, but this time Seahorse stopped them.

He said, "Guys wait! Why don't we go up to Shark and talk to him? My Daddy told me we should give everyone a chance and not judge them so fast."

His friends looked a little worried, but they all agreed that they would go up to the school gates and talk to Shark.

As they got near to the gates, they all started to feel scared.

Dolphin said, "I am too scared to go up to Shark!"

Seahorse said, "I will go over to him. You guys wait here."

Seahorse went up to Shark and said, "Hello Shark."

Shark turned around, and Seahorse got a huge shock!

Shark had been crying.

Seahorse said, "What's wrong, Shark?"

Shark replied, "I have been trying to go to school for two days. I was so excited about making new friends and learning exciting new things, but every day when I come to school, everyone gets scared and swims home. Then the school shuts down."

Seahorse said, "We were afraid you were going to eat us up. That's why we swam away."

Shark smiled and said, "Of course I won't! I am a very friendly and good shark. I always listen to my parents and say 'yes' when they ask me to do something like eat my meals, brush my teeth or go to bed. I am very polite. I always say please and thank you. I am not rude or loud, and I am always kind to everyone."

Seahorse was so happy! He swam back to his friends and told them the good news.

They all went over and met Shark. They introduced themselves, and then they all went into school together.

They all had a great day at school. They learnt loads of exciting new things about plants and also the alphabet. During break-time they all played together and had a lot of fun – after eating their lunch of course!

All the teachers loved Shark because he had such good manners and wasn't naughty.

After school, they all said bye to each other and said they couldn't wait to go back to school the following day.

Seahorse went home and told his parents about the fantastic day they had at school. He said to his dad, "You were right, Daddy. Shark turned out to be lovely, and we had a great day."

Daddy Seahorse said, "What did I tell you! You should always give everyone a chance before judging them."

Seahorse smiled and couldn't wait to go back to school the next day.

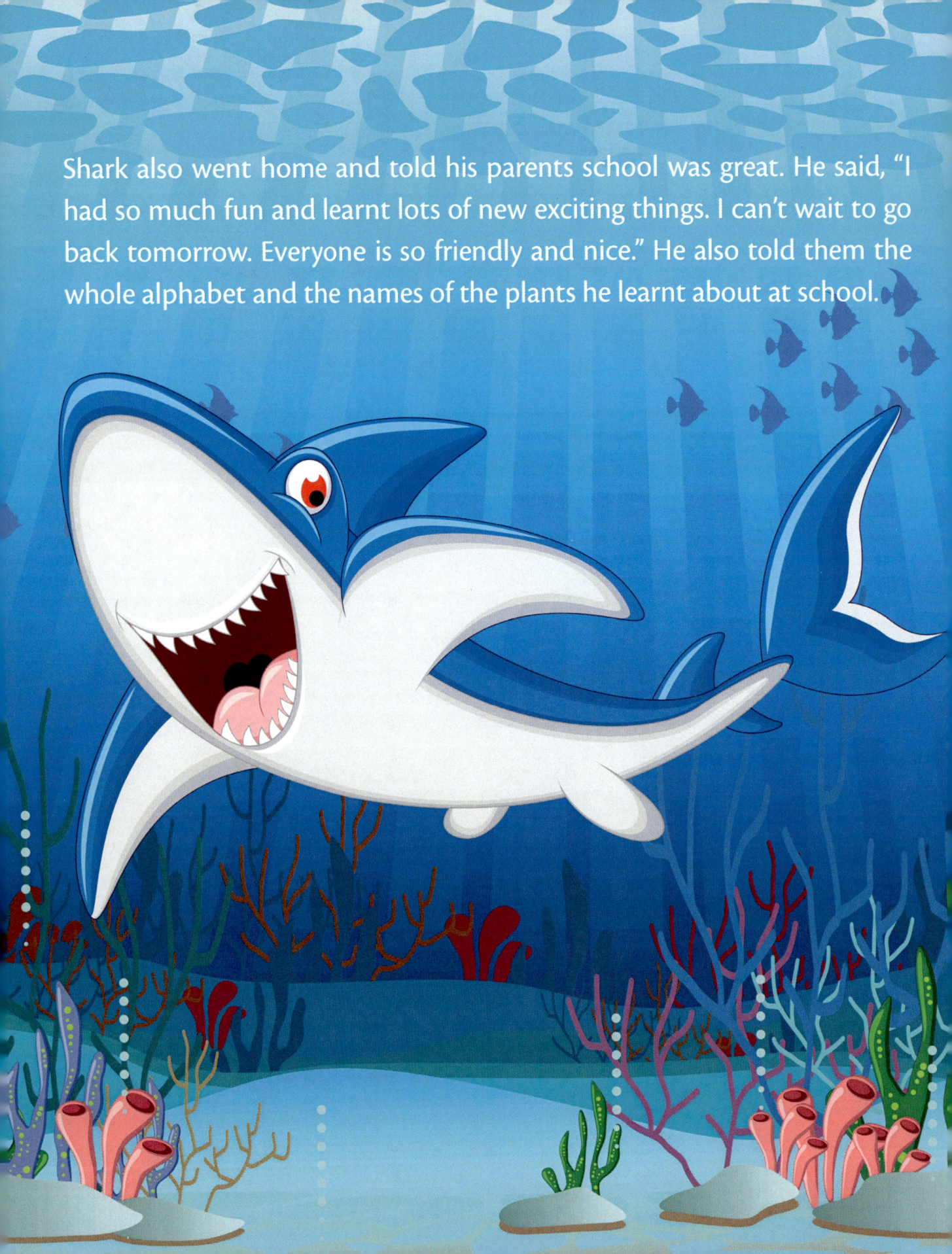

Shark also went home and told his parents school was great. He said, "I had so much fun and learnt lots of new exciting things. I can't wait to go back tomorrow. Everyone is so friendly and nice." He also told them the whole alphabet and the names of the plants he learnt about at school.

Shark's parents were so happy.

And they all lived happily ever after.

The End

Dear Reader,

If you enjoyed reading this book, would you kindly post a short review of the publication on Amazon or whatever book seller site you purchased from. Even one or two lines would be great. Your feedback will make all the difference to getting the word out about this book.

To leave a review on Amazon, type in the book title and go to the book page. Please scroll to the bottom of the page to where it says 'Write a Review' and then submit your review.

Thank you in advance for your kindness.

Made in the USA
Las Vegas, NV
17 November 2020